D1261446

Art Smart

DRAW IT!

Wendy Walker

QEB Publishing

Editor: Lauren Taylor
Design: Tall Tree Ltd www.talltreebooks.co.uk
Illustrator: Tom Connell

Copyright © QED Publishing 2012

Published in the United States by
QEB Publishing, Inc.
3 Wrigley, Suite A
Irvine, CA 92618

www.qed-publishing.co.uk

A CIP record for this book is available from the
Library of Congress.

ISBN 978 1 60992 276 4

Printed in China

Picture credits
(t=top, b=bottom, l=left, r=right, c=center, fc=front cover, bc=back cover)
Mark Winwood: 6cr, 6bl, 7tr, 7c, 7bl, 19cl
Philip Wilkins: 2br, 4cl, 4br, 5tr, 5cl, 5br, 8cl, 8br, 9tr, 9cl, 9br, 10cr,
10br, 11tr, 11c, 11b, 12tl, 12cr, 12bl, 13tl, 13b, 14cl, 15tl, 15bl, 16cr, 16bl,
17tr, 17cl, 17br, 18bl, 19tr, 19br, 20cr, 20bl, 21tl, 21cr, 21b, 22cr, 22bl,
23tl, 23cr, 23bl, 24cr, 24bl, 25tr, 25cl, 25br, 26tl, 26cr, 26bl, 27tr, 27cl, 27b
Shutterstock: fctl, bctr, 22tr, Alex Moe; fctl, fctc, fccr, bctc, bccr, 3br,
16bl, 30cl, Nattika; fctc, bctl, 3tl, 6tr, 6bl, 7br, George Filyagin; fctr,
fcbr, 25tr, de2marco; fcc, fccr, bcc, 19tr, 22bc, 31tl, artproem; fccr,
Kuzmin Andrey; fcbl, 3bl, 4cl, 28tc, Olha Ukhal; fc, bccl, 3bl, 4cr,
22tc, 28tl, Picsfive; 3cr, 12t, 13b, 14tr, 20tr, 20bl, 26tr, Kitch Bain;
3br, 4tr, 8br, 17tr, 20tc, 22bl, 30tl, Evyatar Dayan; 8tr, 10cl, 20tl, 26tr,
31tc, Alexandr Makarov; 8cr, 31tr, BonD80; 10tr, 14cr, shutswis;
15cr, 31cr, magicoven; 29tr, advent

Note to Adults:
Some children might be able to
do some or all of these projects
on their own, while others might
need more help. These are
projects that you can work on
together, not only to avoid any
problems or accidents, but also
to share in the fun of making art.

At the top of the page for each project you will
find this handy key. It will tell you the difficulty
level to expect from each project:

Quick Creative Fix -
These projects are quick, easy and perfect for
a beginner.

Sharpen Your Skills -
Confident with your beginner skills? Move onto
these slightly tougher projects.

Ready For a Challenge -
For a challenging project you can really get
stuck into.

Creative Masterpiece -
Think you can tackle the toughest drawing
projects? Have a go at these.

CONTENTS

FADING SHADING

Perfect your shading skills to create this layered pencil, moonlit landscape.

YOU WILL NEED:

- Selection of drawing pencils
- Letter-sized paper
- A penny

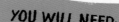

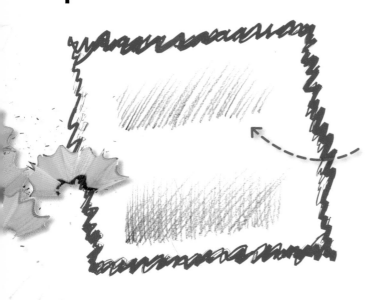

1 Practice shading with the side of a pencil point to make long strokes in the same direction. Try a soft pencil like a B or 2B, and don't press too hard. Add another layer over the first set, but going in a different direction.

2 Build up more layers of pencil in different directions and with strokes of different length until you feel confident shading from dark to light.

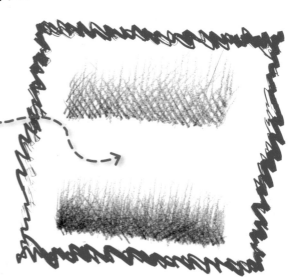

3 Draw out a 5 x 5 inch square. Draw some light, simple pencil lines from one side of the square to the other. Your lines might suggest sky, land, water, trees or buildings. Draw around a penny to make the moon.

4 Begin your fading shading in the bottom shape. The fade can go upwards or downwards.

5 Make sure you shade each section in the same direction so that each one contrasts against the one next to it.

Sharpen your pencil regularly to keep your shading even.

FROTTAGE BUTTERFLIES

Build layers of textures and colors. Frottage comes from a French word, and means "rub."

1 Choose a textured surface and place a sheet of paper over it. With a colored pencil or crayon, make a rubbing by coloring firmly over it with strokes in the same direction.

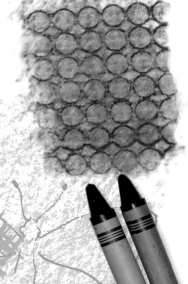

2 Experiment with all of your surfaces, using different colors and how firmly you make the rubbing.

3 Prepare a new sheet of paper with a background layer of one type of rubbing. Draw the outline of a butterfly with an HB pencil. You could trace a photograph of a butterfly, if you like.

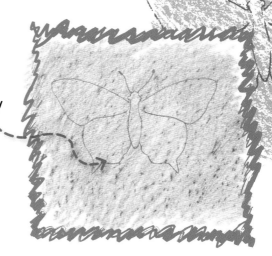

4 Add another layer of a different texture in a different color inside the wing shapes.

5 Have fun inventing the patterns and strong colors of your butterfly. Fill in all the shapes, using colored pencils for the finer detail.

Netting, feathers, leaves, burlap, wood grain, wallpaper... you can make rubbings with so many things!

JUNGLE LINES

YOU WILL NEED:

- Paper
- Black fineliner pens in various thicknesses
- HB pencil

Create a jungle full of exotic animals and plants. All you need is pencils and pens.

1 Practice drawing some lines with your markers. Experiment with creating textures and patterns. What type of lines make things appear closer or further away?

2 With a pencil, lightly draw the outlines of leaf and plant shapes. These are planning lines that you will not see on your final drawing.

3 Add and overlap more jungle shapes at the bottom of the picture. This will form the foreground of your scene. Add tree trunks to the background too.

4 Look at the spaces you have left and imagine where you can place animals, hiding or peering out from behind the jungle plants. Keep adding more plants or flowers until it becomes a dense and exotic rain forest.

5 Redraw your planning lines using black fineliner pens. Look at your experiments from step **1** to help you decide which kinds of lines work best to describe the different areas of your jungle.

COOL CATS

Capture these cool, colorful characters for fun stickers.

1 Using the heavy drawing paper, draw and cut out a template of a cat's head to use over and over again.

2 Using sheets of different colored sticker paper, draw around your template and cut out the cat's head shapes.

3 On a separate sheet of paper, practice drawing different faces and expressions.

4 Choose the faces you like best and draw them onto your cutout heads.

5 You can stick your cool cats wherever you like! The repeat design would also make a brilliant wrapping paper.

Using a simple template is a quick way to make repeat patterns.

BLAST OFF!

Use simple perspective drawing to launch a rocket into space!

YOU WILL NEED:
- Paper
- HB pencil
- Ruler
- Eraser
- Colored markers

1 Begin by drawing a dot and a circle, some distance apart, using a pencil. You will need to erase them later.

2 Using a ruler, draw planning lines against the top and bottom curve of the circle to the dot. You will see a tube shape forming.

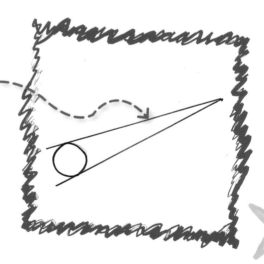

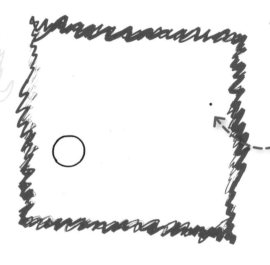

3 Draw another circle for a curved end to the tube shape, halfway down your planning lines.

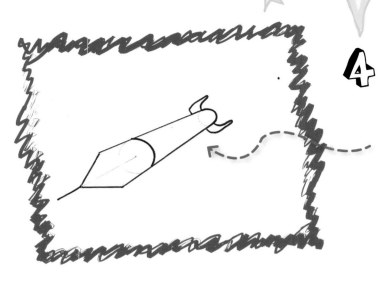

4 Turn the tube into a rocket by adding a triangular tip and some wings. Erase the planning lines and strengthen the lines you want to keep with darker pencil or pen. The dot becomes a planet millions of light years away.

5 Use your imagination. Add detail to build up your scene in color.

Sweeping lines and curves will add speed and movement to your drawing.

MAIL IT!

Send your postcard creations across the world or simply mail them to yourself.

1 Decide on the type of postcard you want. It could be old and written on, or blank so you can start from scratch.

2 Think about how you want to decorate your postcard. You could decide to say "Hello" in lots of different languages.

hola

hi

hello

salut

konnichawa

hello

bonjour

ciao

3 You could use old envelopes with patterns, stamps, postmarks and torn edges to make a collage. Overlap your collage pieces to make a patchwork and think about how you want to fill in the spaces.

4 Arrange your collage before gluing it all into place on your postcard. You can use markers or stickers to add more color and interest.

Start a collection of scraps of any items that you find interesting to use for collage creations.

To: Alex Taylor
123 Any Street
Village Town
AAA 1BB

5 Make another collage for the other side of your postcard, and don't forget to leave space for the address. Now all you need to do is mail it to the lucky recipient!

LEOPARD SPOT PHOTO FRAME

Animal prints can make really great patterns and are easier to draw than you might think!

1 Draw a 5 x 5 inch (12 x 12 cm) square on your paper or card. Choose the colors for your fur base. Yellows, oranges, reddish browns and dark browns will work well. Working with the lightest color first, begin to overlap your colors loosely, with long, fast strokes, to suggest a furry texture. Fill the whole square with your colors.

2 Practice drawing leopard spots. No two spots are exactly the same. They almost look like wiggly "O" and "C" letter shapes.

3 Carefully copy the spots onto your colored square and fill them in with a dark color.

4 Dip your finger into a bowl of water and use it to print furry "splatter" effects on your spots. When it is completely dry, use the colored pencils to add a final layer of squiggly, furry texture.

5 Cut out your colored square and stick your photograph in the center with a few drops of glue. Slide your picture carefully into the front of the CD case. It should fit perfectly and the frame will stand up on its own when it is left open.

What other types of animal print could you make?

MUSICAL DOODLES

Doodling to music stops you thinking too hard and allows your imagination to break free.

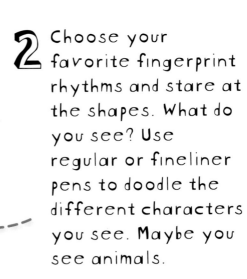

1 Put on your music and take a moment to clear your mind. When you feel ready, press your fingers onto the ink pad and make fingerprint rhythms that dance across the page. Do the rhythms you make change if you change the style of music?

2 Choose your favorite fingerprint rhythms and stare at the shapes. What do you see? Use regular or fineliner pens to doodle the different characters you see. Maybe you see animals.

3 Add as much details as you like to your doodles, using a pencil first if you need more confidence.

4 Try varying the thickness of the lines you make to add more impact. Would dancing people be drawn with bolder lines than fluttering birds?

5 You could also try doodling on different types of paper. There's no limit to the different creations you can make when you free your imagination!

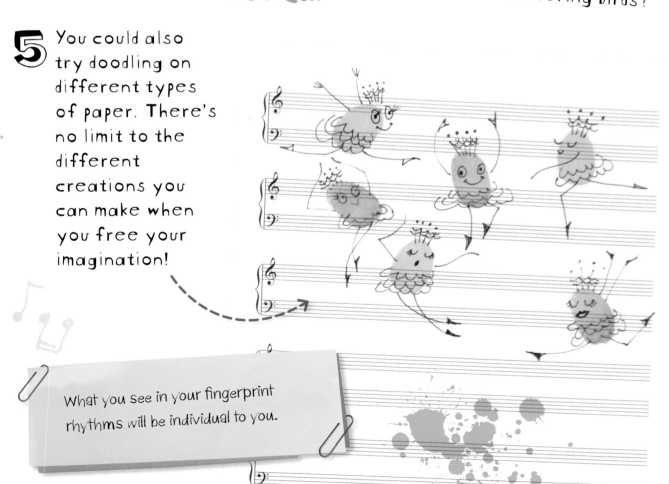

What you see in your fingerprint rhythms will be individual to you.

SPIRAL ART

What creative pictures can you make using only spirals?

YOU WILL NEED:
- Heavy drawing paper
- HB pencil
- Black fineliner pen
- Colored markers

1 Practice drawing spirals using a pencil. They can be loose or tightly curled.

2 Add a simple head and tail, and you have a snail with a spiral shell. Color your snail with markers, giving the spiral a shell pattern

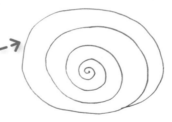

20

3 Use your imagination and find out what other pictures you can make using spirals. Always start with a simple spiral and see where you go from there.

4 Once you have found your favorite spiral drawings, you can build up a scene of spirals. Here, spiral snails are crawling among spiral trees and plants. Color your drawing to bring your scene to life.

Coloring spirals with patterns will make each one look different.

UP AND DOWN FACES

Facial expressions are always changing. **Our** faces can light **up** with joy or hang **down** with sadness.

YOU WILL NEED:

- HB pencil
- Paper
- Black fineliner pen
- Eraser

1 Begin with an oval shape for a head. Find the middle of the oval and add two lines to make a cross. This shows where your features will be drawn.

2 To draw a happy face, mark lines for the eyes that go upwards at the corners on the eye line and a mouth that curves upwards. Add the eyebrows, eye shapes and lips.

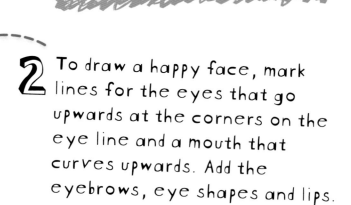

3 Adding cheekbones and dimples will make the smile even stronger. Ears, nose and hair will complete the face.

4 Now make another face in the same way, but make the lines of the eyes and mouth go down at the corners.

5 Use a fineliner pen to strengthen your drawn lines and then erase the unwanted planning lines.

Making the angles more extreme will make an extremely happy or sad face!

23

SAY IT WITH FLOWERS

Create flowers with glitter glue and pastels for a special gift card.

1 Before you begin your design, practice simple flower structures, by studying real flowers. Choose the flower shape you like best and draw its outline lightly with pencil to fit snugly onto your paper or card. Keep the shapes in your drawing really simple.

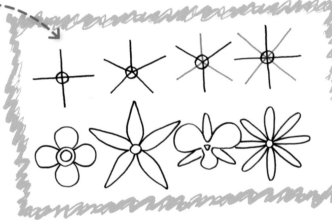

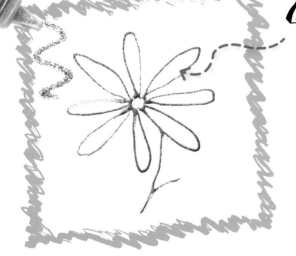

2 Draw over the pencil lines with the glitter glue. Touch the tip of the glue bottle directly onto the paper. Give a little squeeze and let the glue flow in an even line. Pulling the glue bottle towards you is always better than pushing it away from you. Let the glue dry completely.

3 Choose two different colored pastels that will blend well together. One should be a dark color and the other lighter. Working from the center of the flower, add a little of the dark color inside each of the petal shapes, then add the lighter color to half fill each of the petals. Overlap the colors slightly.

4 Carefully blend your colors with a clean finger or a cotton ball, ensuring that the color stays inside the shapes and fades gradually out to the ends of the petals. You can add extra details with the edge of a pastel. Fix your drawing with hair spray or artist's adhesive so that it doesn't smudge.

5 To make your drawing into a gift card, you will need to fold your letter-sized paper in half and carefully glue your drawing onto the front.

Draw a stem with multiple flowers on it, and color them in the same way.

MICROSCOPIC ART

The world looks very different at a microscopic level. If you had microscopic eyes, what treasures would you find?

1 Begin with a single dot which will begin your "microbe." Make your microbe grow "legs" with lines. Keep it simple to begin with by only using four legs. Then add more dots to the ends.

2 Expand your microbe from these new dots.

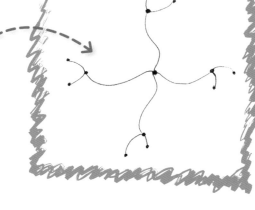

3 Keep adding and growing more legs from each dot. Make your microbe as big as you like.

4 Go back to the middle dot and begin to invent the body of your microbe.

5 Use your imagination to let it grow and grow, then add color to bring life to your drawings.

Fill your paper with microscopic designs. What will your dots and lines become?

MATERIALS

drawing pencil

wax crayons

Drawing Pencils

An HB pencil is recommended to begin with and then try B and 2B for softer shading. Don't try to shade with an H pencil as it is too hard. "H" pencils get harder as the numbers go up, and "B" pencils get softer as the numbers go up.

Colored Pencils

Colored pencils come in a huge variety of colors. Generally they are similar in hardness, but soft ones that can be smudged and blended are available too.

colored pencils

Watercolor pencils

Watercolor pencils look similar to colored pencils, but they are soluble in water, which will give drawings a watercolor effect. You can dip them in water before drawing or color as normal and then brush water over the top.

Wax Crayons

Wax crayons are sticks of colored wax. They come in many colors and are great to use for rubbings as they are typically very blunt, which is good for shading large areas of color. They are also waterproof, so you can paint over the top and the wax color will show clearly through and will not run.

Inks

Drawing inks can be bought in small bottles. They can be diluted with water and applied with a brush or pen. Interesting effects can be created by dropping small blobs of ink onto wet paper and letting them flow. An ink pad is good for fingerprinting and can be made easily with a small piece of sponge lightly soaked with ink.

inks

Pens and Markers

There are many different kinds of pens and markers available in different thicknesses and colors. Try experimenting with as many as possible to create lines, shading, textures and patterns.

For detailed work try fineliner pens in sizes 0.1mm, 0.3mm, 0.5mm, 0.7mm. For thicker marks try markers with thicker tips.

Permanent markers are generally resistant to rubbing and water, but won't wash off most surfaces so you have to be very careful with them.

markers

fineliner pen

permanent marker

Drawing Paper

Drawing paper is an excellent choice for pencil and pen drawings. It comes in different weights and will take paint, ink, markers and pens very well.

drawing papers

Colored and Textured Paper

Paper can be bought in many textures and colors. Drawing on different colours and textures can give your drawings different effects. Different papers are also great to use for collages.

colored and textured paper

Glue

White glue is a widely-used, safe type of glue which is great for sticking paper and cardstock. It is sometimes called PVA (polyvinyl acetate) or school glue. White glue often comes in a squeeze bottle with a nozzle which makes it very clean and easy to use.

white glue

Glitter Glue

Glitter glue can also be bought in a bottle with a fine nozzle and is suitable for drawing fine lines.

glitter glue

TECHNIQUES

Tips on Cross-hatching

1. Keep your pencil well sharpened and try not to grip it too tightly. Begin with simple strokes all in the same direction, lifting the pencil up between each stroke.

2. Make long, light strokes with the side of the pencil point. Don't press too hard. If the strokes are too short they begin to look like furry caterpillars.

3. Make another layer of shading over the first in a different direction.

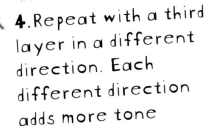

4. Repeat with a third layer in a different direction. Each different direction adds more tone to the shading, and makes it progressively darker and darker.

5. Velvety strokes can be used to finish off areas of shading. Glide the pencil back and forth very lightly over the darkest areas.

7. To make furry strokes, try holding the pencil the long way from its point. Hold it loosely and wiggle it across the paper.

Shading
Lines or other marks used to show gradual changes of color or darkness.

Texture
The appearance and feel of a surface.

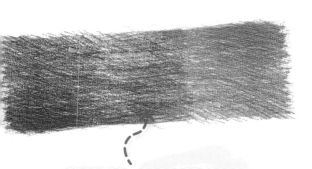

Color Blending
You can use the cross hatching method to overlap and blend colored pencils together.

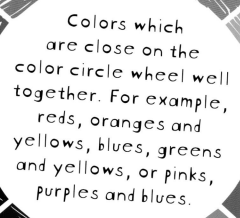

Colors which are close on the color circle wheel well together. For example, reds, oranges and yellows, blues, greens and yellows, or pinks, purples and blues.

Collage
A collage may include newspaper clippings, pieces of fabric, bits of colored or hand-made papers, portions of other artwork or words, photographs and other objects. These can be glued onto paper or canvas in an arrangement of your choice.

Frottage
In frottage the artist takes a pencil or other drawing tool and makes a "rubbing" over a textured surface. The drawing can be left as is or worked into.

Frottage can be made by laying sheets of paper over the surface and then rubbing over them with a soft pencil. It is best to keep the pencil lines in the same direction and to use the side of the point.

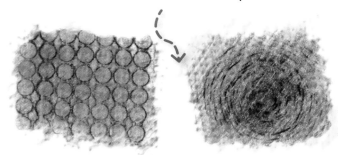

Perspective
Perspective rules help artists to draw in such a way as to make objects appear to be 3D. Remember that objects appear to be smaller when they are in the distance.

Experimenting
Trying things out to see what will happen.

31

INDEX